making math visual

Grade 3
Multiplication and Division
Word Problems

created by

Colleen Uscianowski, PhD

edited by

Marshall Maa

LUMINOUSLEARNING

10 9 8 7 6 5 4 3 2

Published by Luminous Learning Inc, New York
Orders: www.luminouslearning.com
info@luminouslearning.com

ISBN 978-1-939763-27-3

Visit us online: **www.luminouslearning.com**

 facebook.com/LuminousLearning   twitter.com/luminouslearn

youtube.com/user/Luminouslearning    pinterest.com/luminouslearn

www.instagram.com/luminouslearning

 LUMINOUSLEARNING

Table of Contents

Content	Page Number
What teachers and parents need to know about multiplication and division	1
How to use this book	3
Equal groups multiplication problems	4
Array multiplication problems	17
Area multiplication problems	30
Comparison multiplication problems	44
Measurement division problems	56
Fair sharing division problems	69
Mixed multiplication and division problems	82
Appendix: Collection of all multiplication and division problems	92

TEACHERS AND PARENTS:
What you need to know about multiplication and division

In multiplication and division problems, generally there are three pieces of information: the number of **groups**, the number of **items in each group**, and the **total number of items**. When the total is unknown, we call it a multiplication problem. When the number of groups is unknown, we call it a measurement division problem. When the number of items in each group is unknown, we call it a fair sharing division problem.

Type of word problem	Number of groups	Items in each group	Total
Multiplication Example: 5 squirrels are gathering acorns. Each squirrel gathers 9 acorns. How many acorns do they gather in total?	✓	✓	?
Measurement Division (also called Repeated Subtraction) Example: Each squirrel gathers 9 acorns. In total, the squirrels gather 45 acorns. How many squirrels are there?	?	✓	✓
Fair Sharing (also called Partitive Division) Example: 5 squirrels are gathering acorns. In total, they gather 45 acorns. How many acorns has each squirrel gathered?	✓	?	✓

MULTIPLICATION

In this book, children will encounter the following four types of multiplication problems: equal groups, arrays, area problems, and comparison problems.

Equal groups problems: Equal groups form the core of multiplication, and these are likely the first kind of problem you imagine when you think of multiplication. In equal groups problems, we divide things fairly into groups.

For example, "Each bag of pretzels holds 9 pretzels. If there are 6 bags, how many pretzels are there altogether?" In this problem, we know the number of groups (6 bags) and the number of items in each group (9 pretzels). In multiplication problems, it's important for children to understand that each group needs to have the same number of items. We can multiply the number of groups by the number of items in each group to find the product, or the total number of pretzels.

Teaching tip: To solve an equal groups problem, you can draw circles to show the groups. You can draw the item being counted inside the circles.

Array problems: We represent an array problem by creating a rectangular arrangement of circles or dots in rows and columns. The total number of objects in the array tells us the product, or the answer to the multiplication problem.

For example, "We want to arrange the birthday candles on the cake in 4 rows with 3 candles in each row. How many candles do we need?" In this problem, we have items (candles) set up in rows and columns. We can draw an array with 4 rows and 3 columns, then skip count or use repeated addition to find the total number of candles.

Teaching tip: Arrays are very helpful for teaching the commutative property. Students can visualize how 4 x 3 gives you the same product as 3 x 4.

Area problems: Area problems are similar to array problems because we can create a rectangular visual representation of the problem. In area problems, we use multiplication to calculate the area of a space.

For example, "Maggie is painting a wall. The wall is 8 feet long and 7 feet high. How many square feet of space does Maggie need to paint?" Area is measured in square units, such as square inches or square feet. A square unit is 1 unit wide and 1 unit long. Area is the number of square units that can cover the space, without leaving any gaps.

When we model the problem above, we can divide it into square units. We can draw a rectangle and label it 8 feet long and 7 feet high. The square units remind us of an array with rows (7) and columns (8). Then, we can use multiplication to figure out the total number of square units it takes to cover the wall.

Teaching tip: Although we certainly see them pop up in the middle school curriculum, we use area problems less frequently at the elementary level. You can introduce them sparingly in elementary school to help students see how multiplication can be used in various scenarios. When introducing area problems, you can use square tiles to model how we're interested in the space on the inside. This also helps students to see why we measure area using square units.

Comparison problems: Comparison problems represent a relationship between two quantities.

For example, "Yolanda and Francis go outside to collect leaves. Yolanda collects 7 leaves. Francis collects 4 times as many leaves as Yolanda. How many leaves does Francis collect?" In this problem, we're comparing the number of leaves Yolanda and Francis collect.

Teaching tip: Bar models are useful visuals to use when teaching comparison problems.

DIVISION

We distinguish between two kinds of division problems: measurement division and fair sharing.

Measurement division: In a measurement division, or a repeated subtraction, problem, we know the total number of items and the number of items in each group, but we don't know the number of groups. We need to use the number of items in each group to figure out the total number of groups.

For example, "Each squirrel gathered 9 acorns. Altogether, the squirrels gathered 45 acorns. How many squirrels are there?" We can use repeated subtraction to help us solve this problem: we repeatedly subtract 9 from 45 until we are left with 0. We subtract 9 five times, so there are 5 squirrels.

Fair sharing: In a fair sharing, or partitive, division problem, we know the total number of items and the number of groups but we don't know the number of items in each group. We need to partition the total number of objects into groups to find the number per group.

For example, "5 squirrels are gathering acorns. In all, they gather 45 acorns. How many acorns has each squirrel gathered?" Here we can partition the 45 acorns into 5 groups, so that there are the same number of acorns in each group. We place 9 acorns in each group, so each squirrel has gathered 9 acorns.

HOW TO USE THIS BOOK:

There are 7 sections in this book. Sections 1–4 present multiplication problems. Sections 5–6 present division problems. Section 7 presents mixed multiplication and division problems.

Each section begins with a child-friendly explanation of that type of problem, along with a sample problem. Children should read the explanation and work through the sample problem at the beginning of each section. This will help them solve the subsequent multiplication and division problems.

Students can work through the problems in order. For example, they can solve all of the equal groups problems before moving onto the array problems. Alternatively, you can mix and match. You can assign the pages out of order to give students spiraled review with different types of multiplication and division problems.

EQUAL GROUPS
MULTIPLICATION PROBLEMS

In equal groups problems, we divide items fairly into groups. The problem tells us the number of groups and the number of items in each group. We need to find the total number of items.

To solve an equal groups problem, you can draw circles to show the groups. You can draw the item being counted inside the groups. Make sure each group has the same number of items.

After you draw the groups and the items in each group, you can skip count or use repeated addition to find the total number of items. This tells us the product.

For example:

Each bag of pretzels holds 9 pretzels. If there are 6 bags, how many pretzels are there altogether?

These are my 6 bags. Each bag is a group so I have **6 groups.**

Each group has 9 pretzels so there are **9 items in each group.**

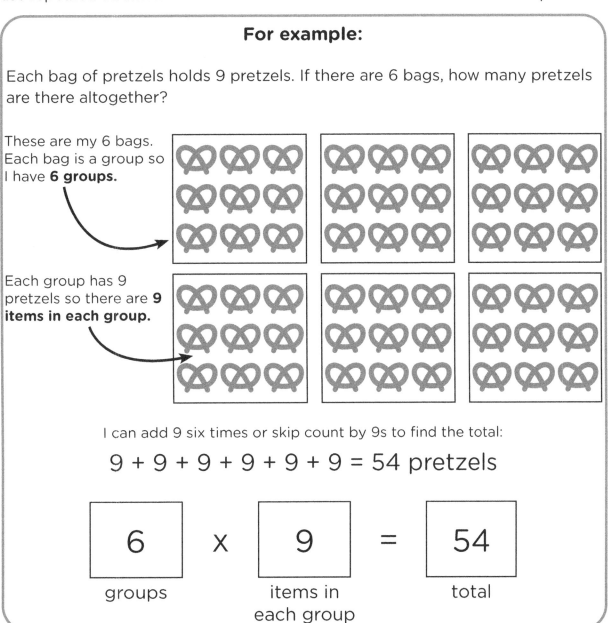

I can add 9 six times or skip count by 9s to find the total:

$$9 + 9 + 9 + 9 + 9 + 9 = 54 \text{ pretzels}$$

6	x	9	=	54
groups		items in each group		total

You have 2 shirts. Each shirt has 1 button. How many buttons in total are on your shirts?

Show your work

groups	X	items in each group	=	total	

Each container holds 1 orange. You buy 6 containers of oranges. How many oranges do you buy?

Show your work

   X      =

groups   items in   total
each group

Name: _____   Date: _____

The butterfly has 2 wings. How many wings do 6 butterflies have in all?

Show your work

 X =

groups   items in   total
              each group

Grandma wants to give each grandkid some coins. She gives 3 grandkids 4 coins each. How many coins does Grandma give away?

Show your work

$$\boxed{} \quad X \quad \boxed{} \quad = \quad \boxed{}$$

groups   items in   total
                each group

You are organizing your sock drawer. You have 9 pairs of socks. Each pair has 2 socks. How many socks do you have?

Show your work

☐ X ☐ = ☐

groups   items in   total
             each group

Name: _____   Date: _____

There are 10 cows on the farm. Each cow has 4 legs. How many legs are there in all?

Show your work

☐ X ☐ = ☐

groups   items in   total
          each group

10

The apple orchard has 5 trees. Each tree has 8 apples. How many apples are there in total?

Show your work

⬚ X	⬚ =	⬚
groups	items in each group	total

There are 3 people in the Johnson family. Each person eats 3 pancakes for breakfast. How many pancakes do the Johnson family eat altogether?

Show your work

$$\boxed{} \times \boxed{} = \boxed{}$$

groups   items in   total
                each group

Name: _____   Date: _____

Each box has 3 muffins. You buy 5 boxes. How many muffins do you buy?

Show your work

groups   X   items in each group   =   total

Name: _____   Date: _____

Each student pays 10¢ to feed the animals. How much money do 8 students pay in total?

Show your work

X

=

| groups | items in each group | total |

You give 7 of your friends 7 crayons each. How many crayons do you give your friends altogether?

Show your work

 X =

groups   items in   total
each group

Each basket has 9 strawberries. You buy 6 baskets. How many strawberries do you buy?

Show your work

$\boxed{}$ X $\boxed{}$ = $\boxed{}$

groups   items in   total
each group

ARRAY
MULTIPLICATION PROBLEMS

In an array problem, items are arranged in rows and columns. The problem tells us the number of rows and columns. We need to find the total number of items.

You can solve an array problem by drawing an array of rows and columns with circles or dots. The total number of items in the array tells us the answer, or the product of the multiplication problem.

For example:

You want to arrange the birthday candles on the cake in 4 rows with 3 candles in each row. How many candles do you need to use?

I made an array with **3 columns** of circles. Columns go up and down.

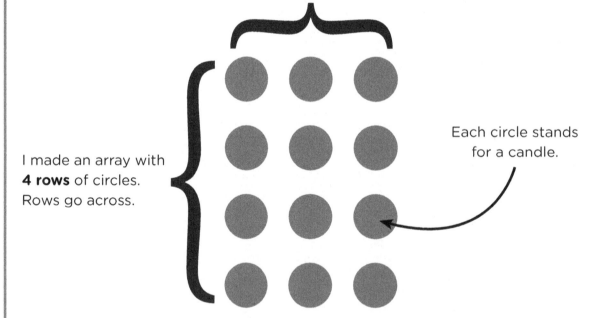

I made an array with **4 rows** of circles. Rows go across.

Each circle stands for a candle.

I can add 4 three times or skip count by 4s to find the total:

4 + 4 + 4 = 12 candles

4	x	3	=	12
rows		columns		total

You buy your friend a box of chocolates. In the box, there are 6 rows of chocolates, with 1 chocolate in each row. How many chocolates are there?

Show your work

X

=

rows   columns   total

You are putting candles on a cake for your friend's birthday. You make 2 rows of candles with 4 candles in each row. How many candles do you use?

Show your work

$$\boxed{} \times \boxed{} = \boxed{}$$

rows   columns   total

You are baking cupcakes. You fill a tray with 5 rows and 2 columns. How many cupcakes do you bake?

Show your work

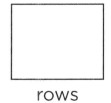 X  =

rows   columns   total

You are decorating your bedroom wall with pictures. You arrange the pictures in 6 columns, with 10 pictures in each column. How many pictures do you hang on the wall?

Show your work

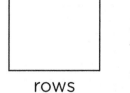 X 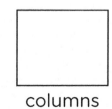 =

rows   columns   total

You plant 6 rows of tulips in the garden. Each row has 5 tulips. How many tulips do you plant?

Show your work

rows	X	columns	=	total

In the crayon box, the crayons are lined up in 5 rows and 9 columns. How many crayons are there?

Show your work

rows   X   columns   =   total

Name: _____   Date: _____

The ice cube tray holds 3 rows of ice cubes and 6 columns of ice cubes. How many ice cubes does the tray hold altogether?

Show your work

X

=

| rows | columns | total |

You are making a quilt with 9 rows. Each row has 9 squares. How many squares are there?

Show your work

$$\boxed{} \times \boxed{} = \boxed{}$$

rows   columns   total

There are 6 rows of trees with 3 trees in each row. How many trees are there in total?

Show your work

	X		=	
rows		columns		total

You plant 4 rows of cucumber seeds. Each row has 4 cucumber seeds. How many cucumber seeds do you plant?

Show your work

$\boxed{}$ X $\boxed{}$ = $\boxed{}$

rows   columns   total

Name: _____   Date: _____

You set up chairs in 7 rows with 4 chairs in each row. How many chairs are there?

Show your work

[ ] X [ ] = [ ]
rows   columns   total

28

Name: _____   Date: _____

You have a carton of eggs. There are 3 rows of eggs with 8 eggs in each row. How many eggs are there?

Show your work

rows	X columns	= total

AREA
MULTIPLICATION PROBLEMS

Area problems involve figuring out the area of an enclosed space. Area means the space inside a boundary, which we figure out by calculating the number of unit squares that cover the surface of the closed figure.

We can solve area problems by creating a rectangular representation of the problem. We then calculate the area of a space by multiplying the width times the length or height.

For example:

Maggie is painting a wall. The wall is 8 feet wide and 7 feet high. How many square feet of space does Maggie need to paint?

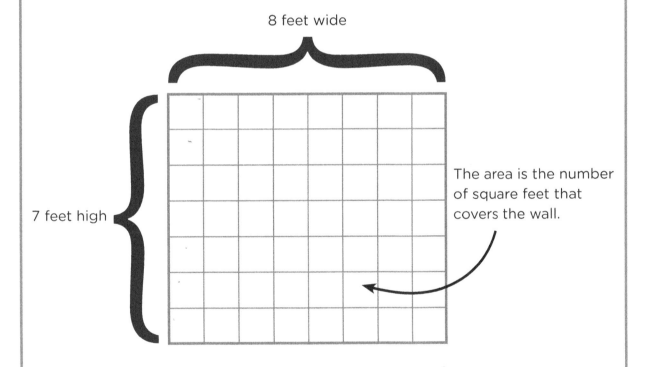

8 feet wide

7 feet high

The area is the number of square feet that covers the wall.

I can add 8 seven times or skip count by 8s to find the area:

8 + 8 + 8 + 8 + 8 + 8 + 8 = 56 square feet

8	x	7	=	56
width		height		square units

Name: _____   Date: _____

You are picking out a new blanket. The blanket is 3 meters long and 1 meter wide. How big is your new blanket in square meters?

Show your work

```
┌───────┐       ┌───────┐       ┌───────┐
│       │   X   │       │   =   │       │
│       │       │       │       │       │
└───────┘       └───────┘       └───────┘
  width           length         square units
```

You want to put new tiles on your patio. Each tile is 1 foot by 1 foot. If the patio is 2 feet wide and 5 feet long, how many tiles will you need?

Show your work

| width | X | length | = | square units |

You are moving your toy box in your room. You measure it to see where it will fit. The toy box is 3 feet wide and 2 feet long. How large is your toy box in square feet?

Show your work

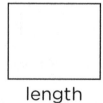 X =

width   length   square units

You are buying a new table. First you measure the table to make sure it will fit in the kitchen. The table is 4 feet wide and 6 feet long. How large is the table in square feet?

Show your work

☐ X ☐ = ☐
width   length   square units

You measure your window to see what size air-conditioner will fit. Your window measures 2 feet wide and 7 feet high. How large is your window in square feet?

Show your work

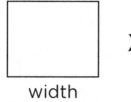 X 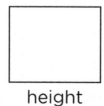 =

width   height   square units

You are building a new desk. The top of the desk is 4 feet long and 2 feet wide. How large is the top of the desk in square feet?

Show your work

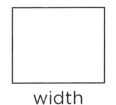

X

=

width   length   square units

You measure the living room floor so you can put down a new carpet. You measure 10 feet long by 7 feet wide. How much carpet will you need to buy in square feet?

Show your work

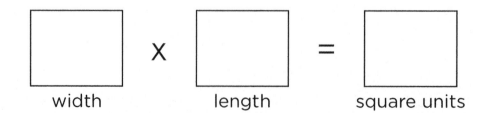

width   X   length   =   square units

You are painting a portrait on a canvas. The canvas is 9 inches wide by 10 inches high. How large is the canvas in square inches?

Show your work

$$\boxed{} \times \boxed{} = \boxed{}$$

width   height   square units

You are decorating the wall with tiles. The wall measures 6 feet wide and 9 feet tall. How large is the wall in square feet?

Show your work

[ ] X	[ ] =	[ ]
width	height	square units

Name: _____ Date: _____

You are planting a garden. The garden is 8 feet long and 5 feet wide. How big is your garden in square feet?

Show your work

| width | X | length | = | square units |

You are making a fort. The fort is 4 meters long by 3 meters wide. How big is your fort in square meters?

Show your work

 X =

width   length   square units

Name: _____   Date: _____

You are building a fence around a pool. The pool is 9 feet wide
and 8 feet long. How large is the pool in square feet?

Show your work

 X =

width   length   square units

COMPARISON
MULTIPLICATION PROBLEMS

Comparison problems show a relationship between two amounts. You are comparing two items or two sets of items.

Bar models are a useful visual aid to help you solve comparison problems.

For example:

Yolanda and Francis go outside to collect leaves. Yolanda collects 7 leaves. Francis collects 4 times as many leaves as Yolanda. How many leaves did Francis collect?

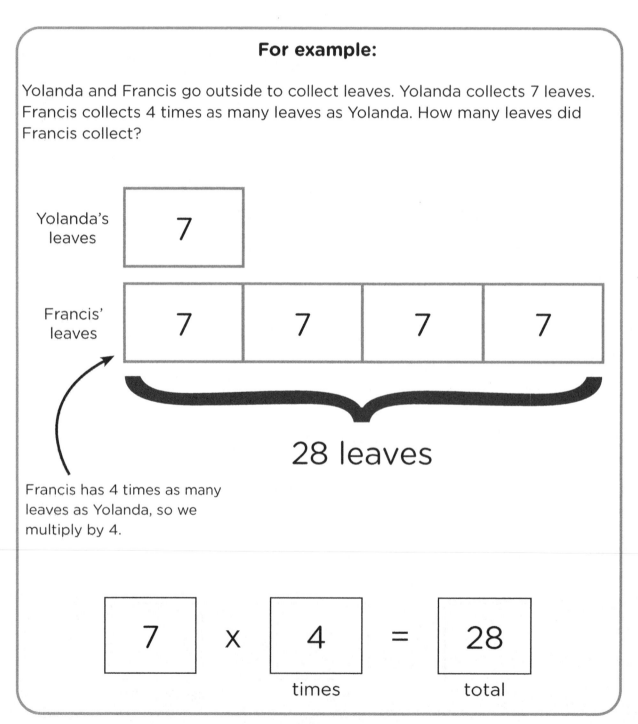

Yolanda's leaves: 7

Francis' leaves: 7 7 7 7

28 leaves

Francis has 4 times as many leaves as Yolanda, so we multiply by 4.

7 x 4 = 28

times   total

Name: _____ Date: _____

A recipe calls for 2 cups of water to make one pot of soup. You want to make twice as many pots of soup. How many cups of water will you use?

Show your work

☐ X ☐ = ☐

times   total

You usually practice playing the piano 2 days a week. Last week, you practiced playing the piano 3 times longer than usual. How many days did you practice the piano last week?

Show your work

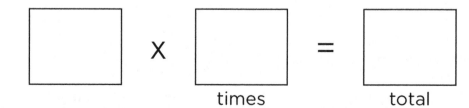

☐ X ☐ = ☐
        times   total

Last month you rode your bike for 5 hours. This month, you rode your bike 4 times as long as last month. How many hours did you ride your bike this month?

Show your work

☐ X ☐ = ☐

times   total

The plant measured 7 inches in height last month. This month, its height grew twice as tall. How tall is the plant now?

Show your work

X ⬜ = ⬜

             times   total

Name: _____   Date: _____

The track team ran 5 miles on Monday. On Tuesday, the track team ran 3 times as many miles. How many miles did the track team run on Tuesday?

Show your work

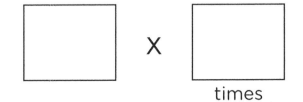

X ☐ = ☐
times   total

Nala the cat weighs 8 pounds. Otis the dog weighs 8 times as much as Nala. How much does Otis weigh?

Show your work

 X 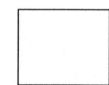 =

                   times   total

Name: _____   Date: _____

You need 8 eggs to make one batch of egg salad. If you want to make 3 times as many batches of egg salad for the picnic, how many eggs will you need?

Show your work

 X 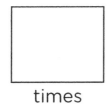 =

times   total

Name: _____ Date: _____

You walk your dog for 10 minutes on Saturday. You walk your dog 5 times as long on Sunday. How many minutes do you walk your dog on Sunday?

Show your work

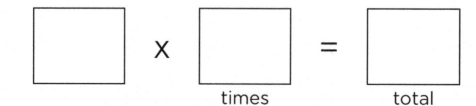

X   times   =   total

Name: _____   Date: _____

You have a puppy that was 6 pounds last month. It has doubled in size since then. How much does your puppy weigh now?

Show your work

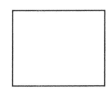 X 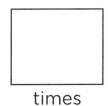 =

times total

Name: _____

Date: _____

The shark swam 7 miles. The whale swam 5 miles longer than the shark. How many miles did the whale swim?

Show your work

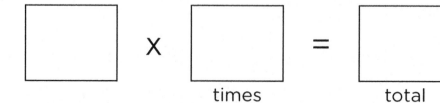

| | X | | = | |
| | | times | | total |

Name: _____ Date: _____

You ate 9 raisins for snack yesterday. Today, you ate 5 times as many raisins as yesterday. How many raisins did you eat today?

Show your work

 X 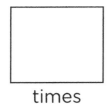 =

times   total

You cut a ribbon that is 4 inches long. Your friend cuts a ribbon that is 10 times as long as yours. How many inches in length is your friend's ribbon?

Show your work

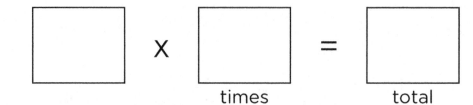

X   =

times   total

MEASUREMENT
DIVISION PROBLEMS

In a measurement division problem, also called a repeated subtraction problem, we know the total number of items and the number of items in each group, but we don't know the number of groups.

We need to use the number of items in each group to figure out the total number of groups. We can use repeated subtraction to help us solve measurement division problems.

For example:

Each squirrel gathered 9 acorns. Altogether, the squirrels gathered 45 acorns. How many squirrels are there?

$$45 - 9 = 36$$

$$36 - 9 = 27$$

$$27 - 9 = 18$$

$$18 - 9 = 9$$

$$9 - 9 = 0$$

We start with the total of 45 and keep subtracting 9 until we have none left. We subtract 5 times so we have 5 groups, or 5 squirrels.

45	÷	9	=	5
total		items in each group		groups

You are wrapping up 6 presents. You will give each person in your family 2 presents. How many family members are receiving presents?

Show your work

	÷		=	
total		items in each group		groups

Some friends are dividing a pack of 18 cards. Each friend gets exactly 9 cards. How many friends are there?

Show your work

[ ] ÷ [ ] = [ ]

total   items in   groups
           each group

You bought 12 toys for your cats. Each cat gets 4 toys. How many cats do you have?

Show your work

total	items in each group	groups

$$\boxed{} \div \boxed{} = \boxed{}$$

Name: _____   Date: _____

You are having a party and are giving out 15 balloons. Each friend gets 3 balloons. How many friends receive balloons?

Show your work

```
┌─────────┐       ┌─────────┐       ┌─────────┐
│         │   ÷   │         │   =   │         │
│         │       │         │       │         │
└─────────┘       └─────────┘       └─────────┘
  total           items in            groups
                 each group
```

Name: _____   Date: _____

You made a batch of 16 muffins. Each friend gets 2 muffins. How many friends receive muffins?

Show your work

$$\boxed{} \div \boxed{} = \boxed{}$$

total   items in   groups
each group

Name: _____   Date: _____

You are collecting 50 skipping stones for you and your friends to use. Each of you will get 5 stones. How many people are skipping stones?

Show your work

$$\boxed{} \div \boxed{} = \boxed{}$$

total   items in   groups
              each group

You are handing out 35 papers to classmates. Each classmate will get 7 papers. How many classmates receive papers?

Show your work

	÷		=	
total		items in each group		groups

Name: _____ Date: _____

You are packing up 30 old toys to give away. You can fit 10 toys in each box. How many boxes do you need?

Show your work

| total | ÷ | items in each group | = | groups |

You are using 20 cherry tomatoes to make a few salads. You put 5 cherry tomatoes in each salad. How many salads are you making?

Show your work

$$\boxed{} \div \boxed{} = \boxed{}$$

total   items in   groups
              each group

A group of octopuses are in the aquarium. You count 72 total limbs. If each octopus has 8 limbs, how many octopuses are there?

Show your work

total	÷	items in each group	=	groups

You are mailing 30 cards. You are mailing 5 of them to each person. How many people are you mailing cards to?

Show your work

☐	÷	☐	=	☐	
total		items in each group		groups	

Name: _____   Date: _____

You are selling 56 kazoos. If you sell them in packs of 7, how many packs of kazoos do you sell?

Show your work

$$\boxed{} \div \boxed{} = \boxed{}$$

total   items in each group   groups

FAIR SHARING
DIVISION PROBLEMS

The second type of division problem is called a fair sharing, or partitive, division problem. In a fair sharing division problem, we know the total number of items and the number of groups, but we don't know the number of items in each group.

We need to separate the total number of objects into groups to find the number of items per group. Start by drawing the number of groups. Then draw circles or dots to show the number of items in each group. Make sure to divide the items fairly, so that there are the same number in each group.

For example:

5 squirrels are gathering acorns. In all, they gathered 45 acorns. How many acorns did each squirrel gather?

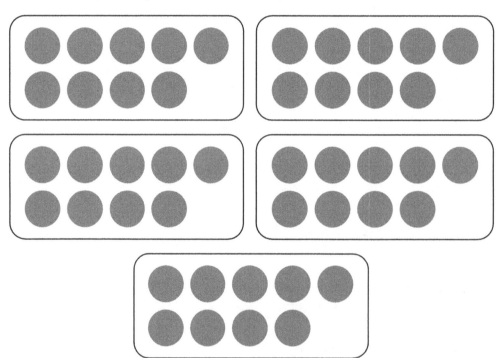

Keep drawing circles until you draw all 45 circles, or acorns. Make sure to put the same number of circles in each group. We have 9 circles in each group. This means each squirrel gathered 9 acorns.

45	÷	5	=	9
total		groups		items in each group

You pass out 20 crayons fairly among 2 classmates. How many crayons does each classmate get?

Show your work

total	÷	groups	=	items in each group	

27 bananas are grouped in 9 bunches. There are the same number of bananas in each bunch. How many bananas are in each bunch?

Show your work

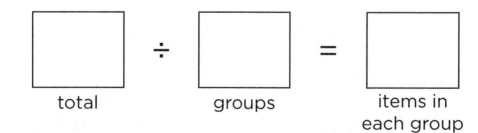

total ÷ groups = items in each group

You plant 25 seeds in 5 pots. There are the same number of seeds in each pot. How many seeds are in each pot?

Show your work

total	÷	groups	=	items in each group

You divide 32 erasers into 4 containers. How many erasers do you put in each container?

Show your work

$\boxed{} \div \boxed{} = \boxed{}$

total   groups   items in each group

The squirrel arranges 21 acorns in 3 piles. Each pile has the same number of acorns. How many acorns are in each pile?

Show your work

| total | ÷ | groups | = | items in each group |

42 dimes are shared equally among 6 friends. How many dimes does each friend receive?

Show your work

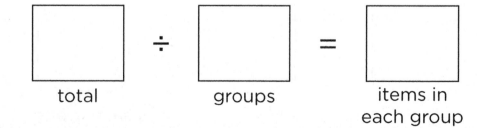

total ÷ groups = items in each group

Name: _____   Date: _____

During your birthday party, you pass out 24 balloons fairly to 6 friends. How many balloons do you give each friend?

Show your work

total	groups	items in each group

$$\boxed{} \div \boxed{} = \boxed{}$$

You bring 70 grapes to school and share them with 7 of your friends at snack time. You give each friend the same number of grapes. How many grapes does each friend get?

Show your work

$$\boxed{} \div \boxed{} = \boxed{}$$

total   groups   items in
                                        each group

At the party, you share 36 cookies fairly with 6 friends. How many cookies do you give each friend?

Show your work

total	groups	items in each group

$$\boxed{} \div \boxed{} = \boxed{}$$

Name: _____   Date: _____

You have 36 stickers. You place them on 4 pages of your sticker book so that each page has the same number of stickers. How many stickers are on each page?

Show your work

$$\boxed{} \div \boxed{} = \boxed{}$$

total   groups   items in
each group

You organize 63 toys fairly in 9 boxes. How many toys do you put in each box?

Show your work

$$\boxed{} \div \boxed{} = \boxed{}$$

total   groups   items in
                              each group

You're playing a game with marbles. You divide 56 marbles fairly into 8 bags. How many marbles do you put in each bag?

Show your work

☐	÷	☐	=	☐
total		groups		items in each group

MIXED MULTIPLICATION AND DIVISION PROBLEMS

In the following problems, you need to figure out whether you should multiply or divide to solve the problem. Choose a strategy that makes sense to help you solve each problem.

Strategies include:

- Drawing groups and items in each group
- Making an array
- Drawing a rectangle to show the area
- Using a bar model
- Using repeated subtraction
- Partitioning the number of items into groups fairly

You can also use skip counting or repeated addition to help you solve multiplication problems. You can use repeated subtraction to help you solve some division problems.

You are collecting 10 bundles of firewood. Each bundle has 2 logs in it. How many logs do you have?

Show your work

The soup recipe says you need 2 celery stalks to make one pot of soup. You want to make 8 pots of soup. How many celery stalks do you need?

Show your work

Name: _____   Date: _____

You are throwing a basketball. You get 3 points per shot and make 7 shots. How many points do you get?

Show your work

You arrange 30 books on 3 shelves. Each shelf has the same number of books. How many books do you place on each shelf?

Show your work

Your friend throws the ball 9 feet. You throw the ball 3 times as far as your friend. How many feet do you throw the ball?

Show your work

You are building a treehouse. It is 7 feet long by 8 feet wide. How big is your treehouse in square feet?

Show your work

You place 4 photos on each page. You fill 9 pages. How many photos do you have?

Show your work

In total, there are 48 buttons on your shirts. Each shirt has 8 buttons. How many shirts do you have?

Show your work

Name: _____   Date: _____

You plant some roses. You plant them in 7 rows with 4 flowers in each row. How many roses do you plant?

Show your work

APPENDIX:
Multiplication and Division Word Problems

Here are all of the multiplication and division problems presented throughout the book. You can cut out these problems and assign them to students individually. For example, you can cut and paste them into students' math journal for students to solve.

EQUAL GROUPS MULTIPLICATION

You have 2 shirts. Each shirt has 1 button. How many buttons in total are on your shirts?

Each container holds 1 orange. You buy 6 containers of oranges. How many oranges do you buy?

The butterfly has 2 wings. How many wings do 6 butterflies have in all?

Grandma wants to give each grandkid some coins. She gives 3 grandkids 4 coins each. How many coins does Grandma give away?

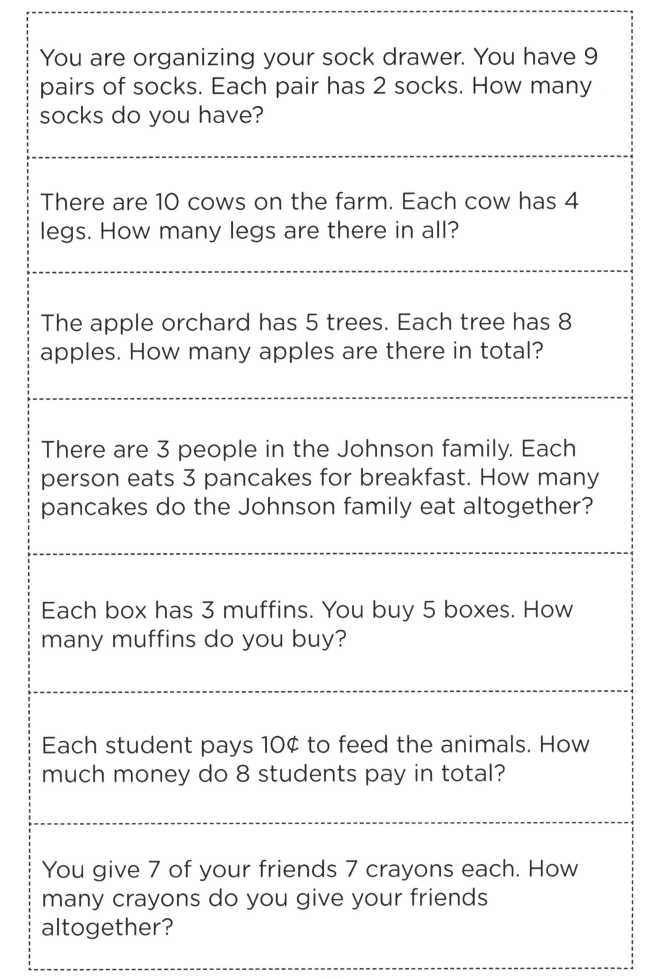

You are organizing your sock drawer. You have 9 pairs of socks. Each pair has 2 socks. How many socks do you have?

There are 10 cows on the farm. Each cow has 4 legs. How many legs are there in all?

The apple orchard has 5 trees. Each tree has 8 apples. How many apples are there in total?

There are 3 people in the Johnson family. Each person eats 3 pancakes for breakfast. How many pancakes do the Johnson family eat altogether?

Each box has 3 muffins. You buy 5 boxes. How many muffins do you buy?

Each student pays 10¢ to feed the animals. How much money do 8 students pay in total?

You give 7 of your friends 7 crayons each. How many crayons do you give your friends altogether?

Each basket has 9 strawberries. You buy 6 baskets. How many strawberries do you buy?

ARRAY MULTIPLICATION

You buy your friend a box of chocolates. In the box, there are 6 rows of chocolates, with 1 chocolate in each row. How many chocolates are there?

You are putting candles on a cake for your friend's birthday. You make 2 rows of candles with 4 candles in each row. How many candles do you use?

You are baking cupcakes. You fill a tray with 5 rows and 2 columns. How many cupcakes do you bake?

You are decorating your bedroom wall with pictures. You arrange the pictures in 6 columns, with 10 pictures in each column. How many pictures do you hang on the wall?

You plant 6 rows of tulips in the garden. Each row has 5 tulips. How many tulips do you plant?

In the crayon box, the crayons are lined up in 5 rows and 9 columns. How many crayons are there?

The ice cube tray holds 3 rows of ice cubes and 6 columns of ice cubes. How many ice cubes does the tray hold altogether?

You are making a quilt with 9 rows. Each row has 9 squares. How many squares are there?

There are 6 rows of trees with 3 trees in each row. How many trees are there in total?

You plant 4 rows of cucumber seeds. Each row has 4 cucumber seeds. How many cucumber seeds do you plant?

You set up chairs in 7 rows with 4 chairs in each row. How many chairs are there?

You have a carton of eggs. There are 3 rows of eggs with 8 eggs in each row. How many eggs are there?

AREA MULTIPLICATION

You are picking out a new blanket. The blanket is 3 meters long and 1 meter wide. How big is your new blanket in square meters?

You want to put new tiles on your patio. Each tile is 1 foot by 1 foot. If the patio is 2 feet wide and 5 feet long, how many tiles will you need?

You are moving your toy box in your room. You measure it to see where it will fit. The toy box is 3 feet wide and 2 feet long. How large is your toy box in square feet?

You are buying a new table. First you measure the table to make sure it will fit in the kitchen. The table is 4 feet wide and 6 feet long. How large is the table in square feet?

You measure your window to see what size air-conditioner will fit. Your window measures 2 feet wide and 7 feet high. How large is your window in square feet?

You are building a new desk. The top of the desk is 4 feet long and 2 feet wide. How large is the top of the desk in square feet?

You measure the living room floor so you can put down a new carpet. You measure 10 feet long by 7 feet wide. How much carpet will you need to buy in square feet?

You are painting a portrait on a canvas. The canvas is 9 inches wide by 10 inches high. How large is the canvas in square inches?

You are decorating the wall with tiles. The wall measures 6 feet wide and 9 feet tall. How large is the wall in square feet?

You are planting a garden. The garden is 8 feet long and 5 feet wide. How big is your garden in square feet?

You are making a fort. The fort is 4 meters long by 3 meters wide. How big is your fort in square meters?

You are building a fence around a pool. The pool is 8 feet long and 9 feet wide. How large is the pool in square feet?

COMPARISON MULTIPLICATION

A recipe calls for 2 cups of water to make one pot of soup. You want to make twice as many pots of soup. How many cups of water will you use?

You usually practice playing the piano 2 days a week. Last week, you practiced playing the piano 3 times longer than usual. How many days did you practice the piano last week?

Last month you rode your bike for 5 hours. This month, you rode your bike 4 times as long as last month. How many hours did you ride your bike this month?

The plant measured 7 inches in height last month. This month, its height grew twice as tall. How tall is the plant now?

The track team ran 5 miles on Monday. On Tuesday, the track team ran 3 times as many miles. How many miles did the track team run on Tuesday?

Nala the cat weighs 8 pounds. Otis the dog weighs 8 times as much as Nala. How much does Otis weigh?

You need 8 eggs to make one batch of egg salad. If you want to make 3 times as many batches of egg salad for the picnic, how many eggs will you need?

You walk your dog for 10 minutes on Saturday. You walk your dog 5 times as long on Sunday. How many minutes do you walk your dog on Sunday?

You have a puppy that was 6 pounds last month. It has doubled in size since then. How much does your puppy weigh now?

The shark swam 7 miles. The whale swam 5 miles longer than the shark. How many miles did the whale swim?

You ate 9 raisins for snack yesterday. Today, you ate 5 times as many raisins as yesterday. How many raisins did you eat today?

You cut a ribbon that is 4 inches long. Your friend cuts a ribbon that is 10 times as long as yours. How many inches in length is your friend's ribbon?

MEASUREMENT DIVISION

You are wrapping up 6 presents. You will give each person in your family 2 presents. How many family members are receiving presents?

Some friends are dividing a pack of 18 cards. Each friend gets exactly 9 cards. How many friends are there?

You bought 12 toys for your cats. Each cat gets 4 toys. How many cats do you have?

You are having a party and are giving out 15 balloons. Each friend gets 3 balloons. How many friends receive balloons?

You made a batch of 16 muffins. Each friend gets 2 muffins. How many friends receive muffins?

You are collecting 50 skipping stones for you and your friends to use. Each of you will get 5 stones. How many people are skipping stones?

You are handing out 35 papers to classmates. Each classmate will get 7 papers. How many classmates receive papers?

You are packing up 30 old toys to give away. You can fit 10 toys in each box. How many boxes do you need?

You are using 20 cherry tomatoes to make a few salads. You put 5 cherry tomatoes in each salad. How many salads are you making?

A group of octopuses are in the aquarium. You count 72 total limbs. If each octopus has 8 limbs, how many octopuses are there?

You are mailing 30 cards. You are mailing 5 of them to each person. How many people are you mailing cards to?

You are selling 56 kazoos. If you sell them in packs of 7, how many packs of kazoos do you sell?

FAIR SHARING DIVISION

You pass out 20 crayons fairly among 2 classmates. How many crayons does each classmate get?

27 bananas are grouped in 9 bunches. There are the same number of bananas in each bunch. How many bananas are in each bunch?

You plant 25 seeds in 5 pots. There are the same number of seeds in each pot. How many seeds are in each pot?

You divide 32 erasers into 4 containers. How many erasers do you put in each container?

The squirrel arranges 21 acorns in 3 piles. Each pile has the same number of acorns. How many acorns are in each pile?

42 dimes are shared equally among 6 friends. How many dimes does each friend receive?

You organize 63 toys fairly in 9 boxes. How many toys do you put in each box?

At the party, you share 36 cookies fairly with 6 friends. How many cookies do you give each friend?

You have 36 stickers. You place them on 4 pages of your sticker book so that each page has the same number of stickers. How many stickers are on each page?

You're playing a game with marbles. You divide 56 marbles fairly into 8 bags. How many marbles do you put in each bag?

During your birthday party, you pass out 24 balloons fairly to 6 friends. How many balloons do you give each friend?

You bring 70 grapes to school and share them with 7 of your friends at snack time. You give each friend the same number of grapes. How many grapes does each friend get?

MIXED MULTIPLICATION & DIVISION

You are collecting 10 bundles of firewood. Each bundle has 2 logs in it. How many logs do you have?

The soup recipe says you need 2 celery stalks to make one pot of soup. You want to make 8 pots of soup. How many celery stalks do you need?

You are throwing a basketball. You get 3 points per shot and make 7 shots. How many points do you get?

You arrange 30 books on 3 shelves. Each shelf has the same number of books. How many books do you place on each shelf?

Your friend throws the ball 9 feet. You throw the ball 3 times as far as your friend. How many feet do you throw the ball?

You are building a treehouse. It is 7 feet long by 8 feet wide. How big is your treehouse in square feet?

You place 4 photos on each page. You fill 9 pages. How many photos do you have?

In total, there are 48 buttons on your shirts. Each shirt has 8 buttons. How many shirts do you have?

You plant some roses. You plant them in 7 rows with 4 flowers in each row. How many roses do you plant?

Made in the USA
Las Vegas, NV
15 November 2021